Martin Taylor's

JAZZ**GUITAR**
SOLOING**ETUDES**

Learn 12 Complete Guitar Solo Studies Over Essential Jazz Standards

MARTIN**TAYLOR**
WITH JOSEPH**ALEXANDER**

FUNDAMENTAL**CHANGES**

Martin Taylor's Jazz Guitar Soloing Etudes

Learn 12 Complete Guitar Solo Studies Over Essential Jazz Standards

ISBN: 978-1-78933-241-4

Published by **www.fundamental-changes.com**

Copyright © 2021 Martin Taylor & Joseph Alexander

Edited by Tim Pettingale

www.fundamental-changes.com

Over 13,000 fans on Facebook: **FundamentalChangesInGuitar**

Instagram: **FundamentalChanges**

For over 350 Free Guitar Lessons with Videos Check Out

www.fundamental-changes.com

Cover Image Copyright: Cover Photo: Jo Hanley, **www.johanley.com**

Special thanks to Douglas Gillespie and Gleneagles Hotel

Contents

About the Authors

Dr Martin Taylor MBE is a virtuoso guitarist, composer, educator and musical innovator.

Acoustic Guitar magazine has called him, "THE acoustic guitarist of his generation." Chet Atkins said that Martin is "One of the greatest and most impressive guitarists in the world," and Pat Metheny commented that, "Martin Taylor is one of the most awesome solo guitar players in the history of the instrument."

Widely considered to be the world's foremost exponent of solo jazz and fingerstyle guitar playing, Martin possesses an inimitable style that has earned him global acclaim from fellow musicians, fans and critics alike. He dazzles audiences with a signature style which artfully combines his virtuosity, emotion and humour with a strong, engaging stage presence.

Martin has enjoyed a remarkable musical career spanning five decades, with more than 100 recordings to his credit. Completely self-taught, beginning at the early age of 4, he has pioneered a unique way of approaching solo jazz guitar that he now breaks down into seven distinct stages in order to teach others.

Martin has penned many tuition books for the guitar including:

Beyond Chord Melody

Walking Bass for Jazz Guitar

Martin Taylor Single Note Soloing for Jazz Guitar

Martin Taylor's Christmas Songs for Jazz Guitar

Martin Taylor's Complete Jazz Guitar Method Compilation

Martin Taylor's Jazz Guitar Licks Phrase Book

Martin Taylor's Advanced Jazz Guitar Licks Phrase Book

Joseph Alexander is one of the most prolific writers of modern guitar tuition methods.

He has sold over 1,000,000 books that have educated and inspired a generation of upcoming musicians. His uncomplicated tuition style is based around breaking down the barriers between theory and performance, and making music accessible to all.

Educated at London's Guitar Institute and Leeds College of Music, where he earned a degree in Jazz Studies, Joseph has taught thousands of students and written over 40 books on playing the guitar.

e is the managing director of *Fundamental Changes Ltd.*, a publishing company whose sole purpose is to eate the highest quality music tuition books and pay excellent royalties to writers and musicians.

undamental Changes has published over 140 music tuition books and is currently accepting submissions from rospective authors and teachers of all instruments. Get in touch via **webcontact@fundamental-changes. m** if you'd like to work with us on a project.

blank page

Introduction from Martin

i and welcome to my *Jazz Guitar Soloing Etudes* book.

his book was conceived after the publication of my previous two jazz guitar licks books. We thought, ouldn't it be great if we could show how my jazz language and phrases are developed over the course a ne? The logical next step was to record me performing solos on common changes and turn these recordings to authentic jazz guitar solo studies.

my previous books, I asked the question, "If you were to visit another country and needed to communicate another language, would it be more useful to be given a dictionary or a phrase book?"

f course, that's an easy answer. If you don't even know the words you need, how on earth would you find em in a dictionary? However, given a phrase book, you can immediately copy the sounds and begin to ommunicate. As you gradually learn more phrases from your book and copy the sounds that people are aking, you'll start to combine them and suddenly you're beginning to speak the language.

his book begins at the point where you've learnt some phrases (don't worry, you don't need to know the ones om the previous books – everything you need is included in the etudes) and you're ready to start having a ore detailed conversation with your music.

ve recorded and transcribed solo studies on the chord changes of twelve of the most important jazz guitar andards. Each study begins where the melody of the tune finishes and picks up with a short phrase based a counter melody – a feature of all good jazz solos. From there I develop those initial fragments through a lo of at least three choruses. Throughout, I've kept an emphasis on developing the melody while introducing hrases and vocabulary from my previous books. See if you can spot them!

he goal is for you to develop your jazz guitar phrasing by copying and playing my language over a series of xtended solos. You'll learn new language, but more importantly you'll get a feel for how to construct a well-alanced, interesting, and above all, musical solo.

ou may be thinking, "But what about the *theory!*" My answer to that is, you didn't learn to speak with a book f grammar in your hand, you copied the people around you. Maybe some theory came a little later when you ere at school and you learnt about adjectives and verbs and iambic pentameter, but I'm sure you were doing wonderful job of speaking before you were introduced to these complex ideas.

n this book, there is no theory! There's just language, phrases and the vocabulary that forms the basis of the ch jazz language. I made a conscious decision *not* to include solo breakdowns here, because I want you to ocus solely on the communication and *voice* of your music.

hese studies are written over some of the most common jazz standards, so you can draw on these ideas at ny jam night. Many jazz songs are written using the same sets of chord changes, so the work you do here ill be instantly applicable to hundreds of tunes. More than that though, the ultimate outcome is to learn how combine phrases and develop your soloing *story* over a period of time and carry your listener on a musical ourney over multiple choruses. Learn my solos as they're written, then experiment to find your own voice.

he Standards Covered in This Book

n this book, you'll learn beautiful solo studies that work on the following standards:

- *All the Things You Are*

- *Softly, as in a Morning Sunrise*

- *Bluesette*

- *Blue Moon*

- *Blue Bossa*

- Jazz Blues

- Rhythm Changes

- *Jersey Bounce*

- *How High the Moon*

- *Georgia On My Mind*

- *On Green Dolphin Street*

- *Emily*

I've chosen these tunes because they represent a good cross section of common chord changes, feels and tempos. I also added in jazz blues and rhythm changes etudes, as these two forms alone cover dozens of standard tunes.

Together, these pieces cover the chord changes you'll constantly encounter as a jazz guitarist, and you'll be learning the language you can use over these important sequences:

- Major to minor II V Is

- Minor ii V i

- I vi ii V turnarounds

- Dominant 7 chords moving in 5ths

- Static dominant 7 chords

- II V sequences descending in semitones

- Static minor 7th chords

- Minor blues

- Jazz blues

These sequences are the backbone of hundreds of jazz standards, and by learning phrases for each one you'll quickly learn to "speak jazz" authentically. As these ideas naturally combine and get rooted into your subconscious, they'll quickly begin to influence the phrases you create yourself when improvising.

get the most out of this book, the first thing to do before learning an etude is to listen to it on repeat away from your guitar. This will help you to focus on the structure and character of the solo. Next, if you can, try listening to the music while following along with the notation in the book. This will help you to get a feel for the *shape* of each phrase on paper. You'll also be able to see how each line develops from one to the next, and you'll be more aware of where I use space to punctuate my phrases.

The next stage is to hum or sing along to the solos, still without your guitar. Learn each phrase, one at a time. Even if you can't sing it perfectly, you'll quickly get the shape of the line in your head and this will make it much quicker when you come to learn it on guitar.

Finally, begin learning the solos. You might want to start with any phrases that really catch your ear, but I'd suggest learning each solo as a complete piece of music. That's how you'll begin to learn to develop longer, meaningful solos.

When you can play each phrase in a chorus, spend time linking them all together before playing along with me on the recording. When you're confident, instead of playing with me, solo over the backing track provided for each chapter. When you're ready, move onto the next chorus of soloing and repeat the steps.

Once you've completed the full solo, begin to add variations of your own to create an original solo using the strong structure provided by my original improvisation.

While you're learning the solos, try to spot the chord sequences listed above. Breaking down the chord movements in each study will help you understand what kind of language I'm using and when.

When you sit down to learn a solo, make a commitment to memorise it. To play anything fluently it needs to become a natural part of you. To memorise a line, break it into small rhythmic chunks of just a few beats and repeat each chunk until you can't get it wrong. Then move on to the next chunk or section and repeat the process. Next, combine the first two sections and play them until they're fluent before adding the third, and so on. Remember, you're not just learning a lick, you're programming yourself with how the language feels.

After a while, your musical brain will want to vary the phrase. Don't fight this! These phrases are just a starting point for you. The aim is to teach you the language so you can form your own unique sentences.

Other than listening to and transcribing the music of the great jazz soloists, a great place to start gathering new language is in my previous two phrase books, **Jazz Guitar Licks Phrase Book** and **Advanced Jazz Guitar Licks Phrase Book**.

As you gradually add more and more phrases to your vocabulary, they'll combine and evolve to create your own voice on the guitar.

Learning the language of jazz is a lifetime process, so approach it with a sense of fun and positive energy. I believe there are no "mistakes" when you play, it's just your subconscious trying to take you to places that your fingers haven't caught up with yet! Listen to the music in your head and work on connecting it to your fingers.

My Soloing Strategy

Years ago, when I used to play live sessions, the band were often presented with a chart for a piece not long before we'd have to play it and perhaps improvise a solo. When you are constantly thrust into a situation like that, you become skilled at quickly breaking down a tune and getting to the heart of the harmony.

I would usually glance over the changes and get the sequence in my mind, noticing any key changes and the main tonal centres. This top-level view would give me an idea of the broad scope of the tune. Then, I'd look at the smaller movements within the piece, at a chord level, noticing the ii V movements and, for instance, wha devices were being used to modulate to other keys.

I tend to think in chords rather than scales, so often I'd quickly play through the tune just outlining the bas note movements, and noting whether chords were major, minor or dominant. This would give me a skeleto framework for the tune when it came to soloing.

I still take a similar approach to playing a standard. I'll take a quick look at the geography of the tune, bu then I like to memorise the progression. I don't want to be looking at, or thinking about, the changes when I'r soloing; I want to be in the moment with the music, focusing on being creative. If you're looking at the chor changes while trying to improvise, it's easy to fall into the trap of chasing the changes, rather than playin melodically.

Once you've got a good feel for the structure of a tune, it's time to solo. Here's how I tend to approac improvising over any jazz standard.

First, I'll listen to the original melody of the tune. We may be very familiar with this, but it was written for reason – because it works! The melody is the strongest part of the tune. You don't leave a concert humming chord progression. Almost all jazz standards were originally vocal songs, which is why they have such strong memorable tunes. I like to listen to the melody and hear what counter melodies it suggests. I think, *wha melodic lines can I play that will really capture the flavour of this piece and build on the original melody* Then, I'll begin to play phrases that function as a counter melody.

If you've read my previous books, you'll know that I think of the melody as the starting point for improvisation so I'll begin to play variations on the counter melody that I created. Soloing by varying the melody gives yo an entire *structure* and *framework* for your solo to exist in, so you'll never get lost in the chord changes. Ver often improvisation is taught in a way that says, "You can play this scale over this chord…" but this is too far removed from what actually happens when jazz musicians start improvising. The more intuitive, melodic approach is to *vary the melody.*

Often, when soloing, you'll hit on a nice line or rhythmic phrase that just works well. When this happens you can take that motif, develop it, and see where the idea leads. Each short variation we play leads to the next one. When I play, everything is led by my ears, but they have been trained by years of listening, copying experimenting and playing. The best way to learn this skill is to listen to the playing of great musicians and recycle their ideas (I always joke with my students that we're helping the planet by recycling!) Even if you don't copy their idea perfectly, listening to the approach of other musicians will help you understand the melodic shapes and rhythmic possibilities you can use.

Variation can transform even the most pedestrian of melodies into a jazz solo that has momentum and tells a story. Once you know the chord changes, forget about them and trust your ears. Concentrate on learning to develop your variations. The goal is to embellish the tune and build into a creative solo. Simply and gradually expand the complexity of the variations until you're playing an exciting solo. The secret is to use smal variations that take the melody somewhere new. If you can do this, your audience with be right there with you As you improve this skill, you will naturally become able to start your solos with more intricate variations and jazzier improvisations.

Finally, don't be afraid to experiment and let your creativity guide you. I can't stress enough that if you know the structure/harmony of the tune inside out, you'll be able to forget about it and just concentrate on playing Often, our best lines emerge when we are relaxed, in the moment, and not overthinking what we're playing.

Have fun!

Martin Taylor, June 2021

Get the Audio

he audio files for this book are available to download for free from **www.fundamental-changes.com.** The
ık is in the top right-hand corner. Click on the "Guitar" link then simply select this book title from the drop-
ɔwn menu and follow the instructions to get the audio.

'e recommend that you download the files directly to your computer, not to your tablet, and extract them
ere before adding them to your media library. You can then put them onto your tablet, iPod or burn them to
D. On the download page there are instructions and we also provide technical support via the contact form.

For over 350 free guitar lessons with videos check out:

www.fundamental-changes.com

Join our active Facebook community:

www.facebook.com/groups/fundamentalguitar

Tag us for a share on Instagram: **FundamentalChanges**

Etude 1

Based on *All the Things You Are*

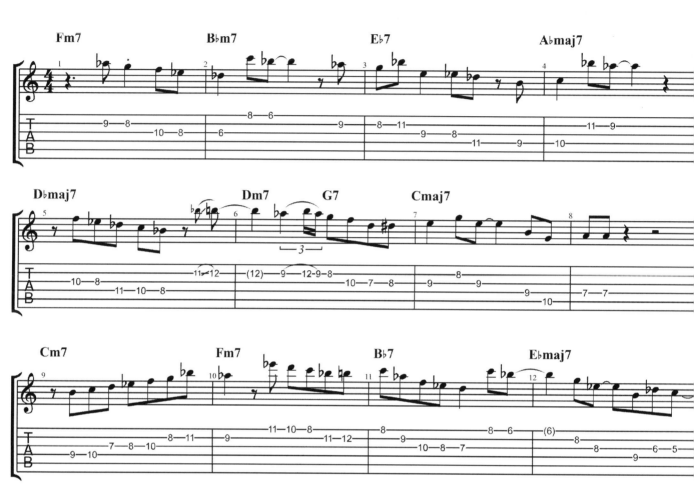

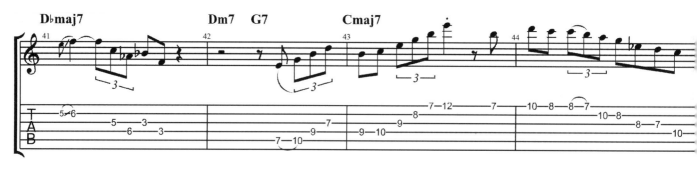

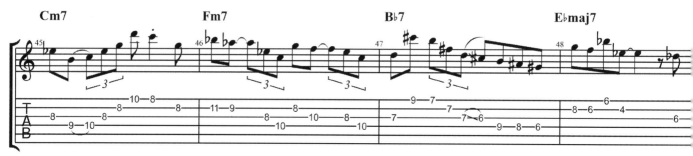

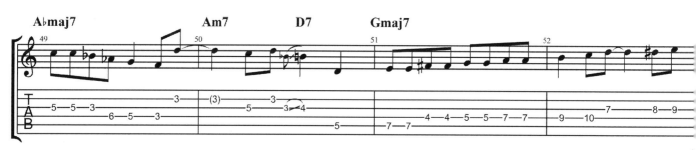

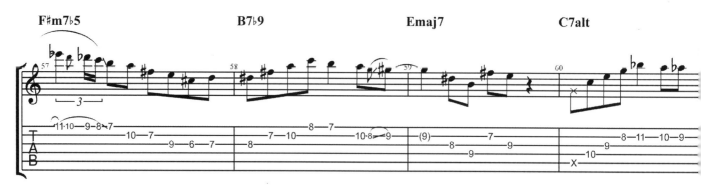

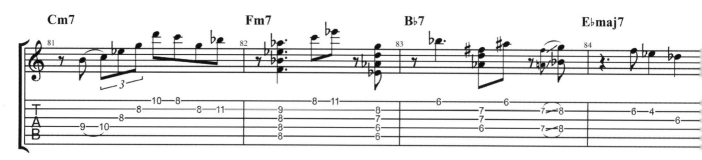

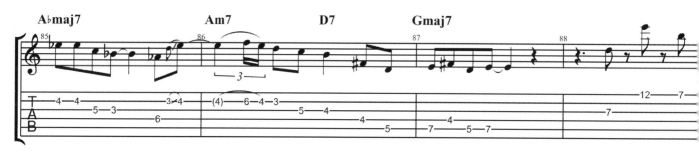

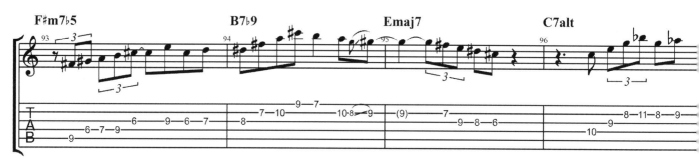

Etude 2

Based on *Softly as in a Morning Sunrise*

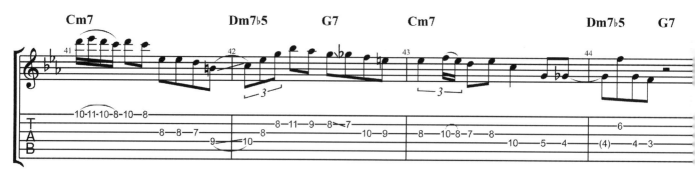

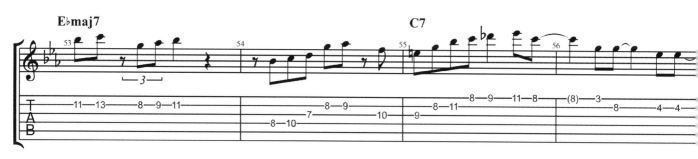

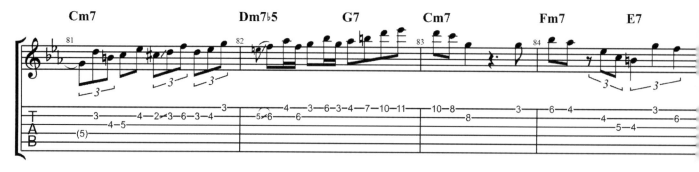

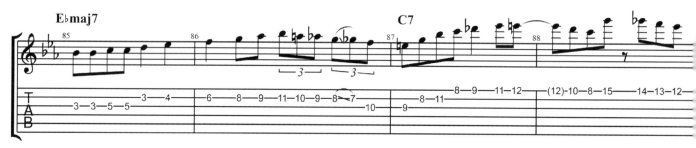

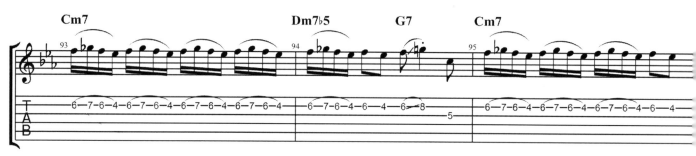

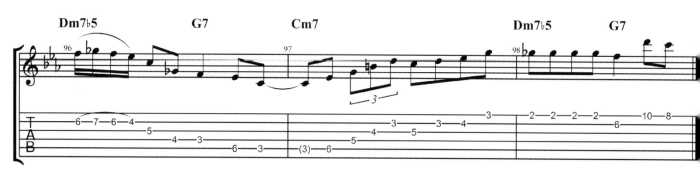

Etude 3

Based on *Bluesette*

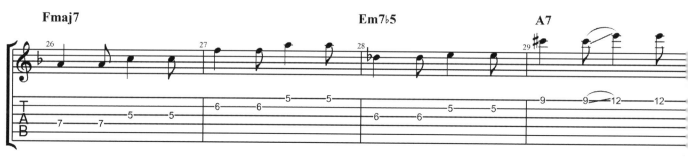

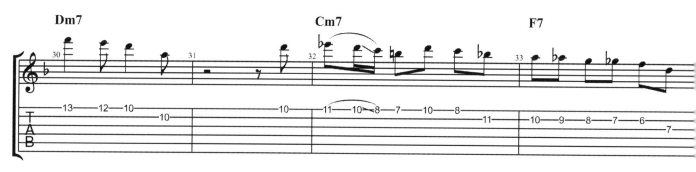

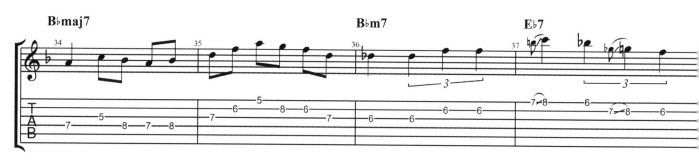

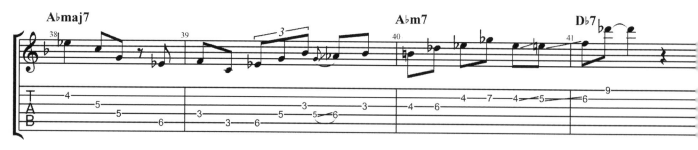

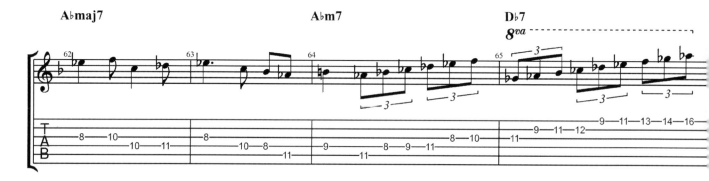

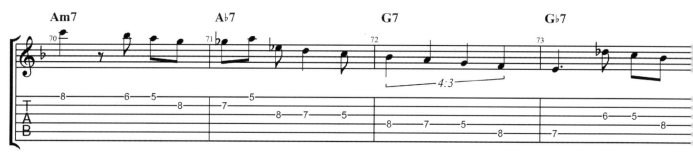

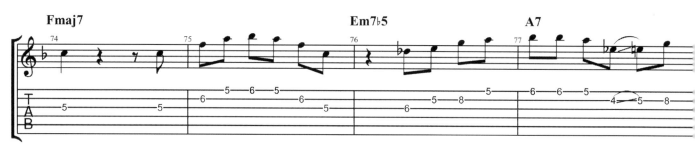

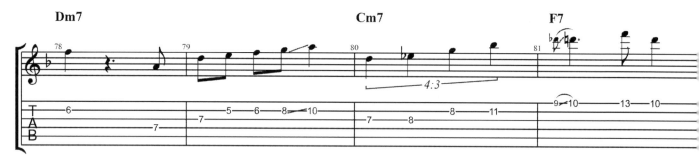

26

Etude 4

Based on *Blue Moon*

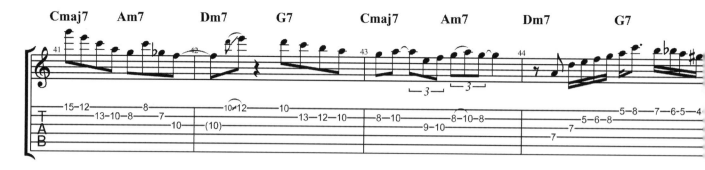

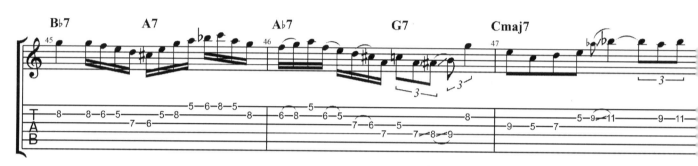

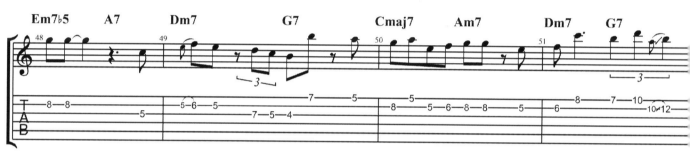

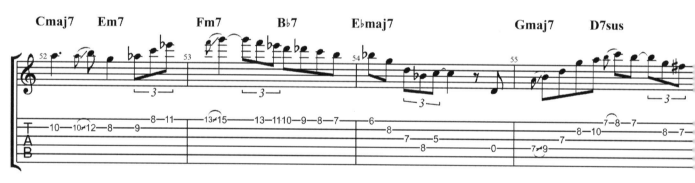

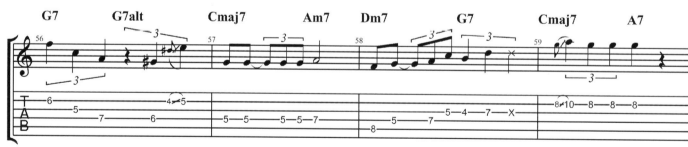

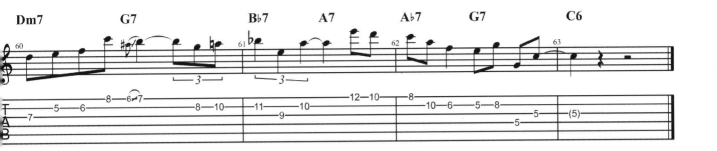

Etude 5

Based on *Blue Bossa*

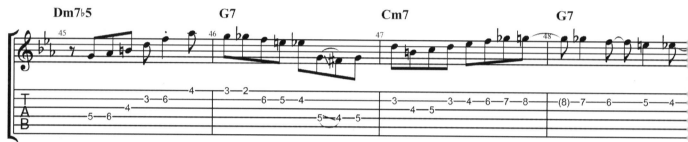

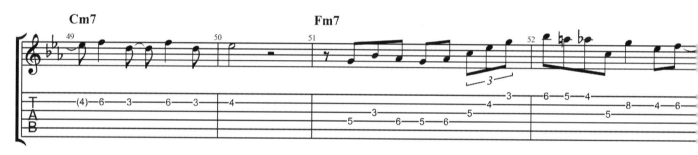

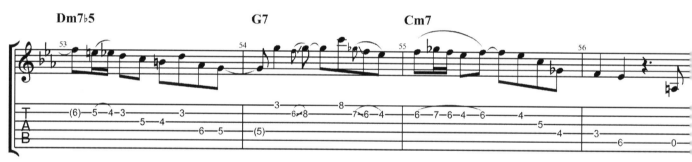

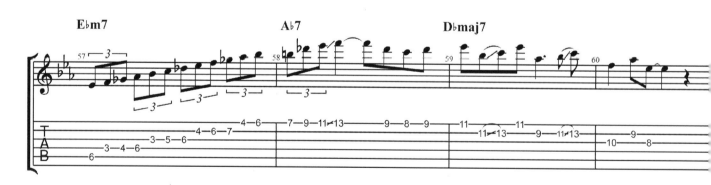

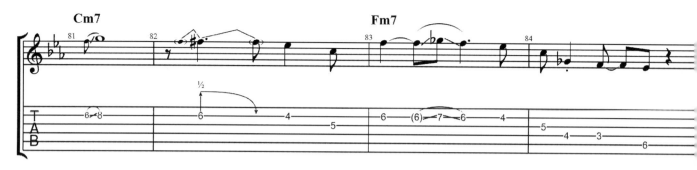

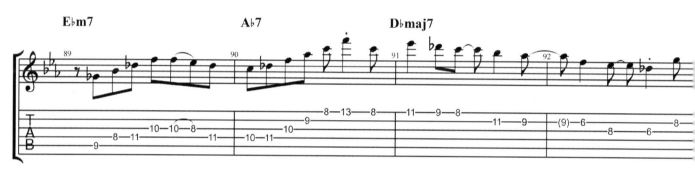

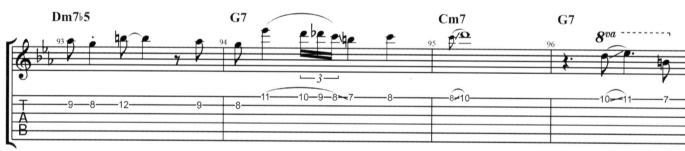

Etude 6

Based on a Jazz Blues

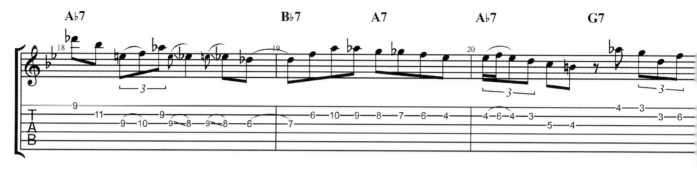

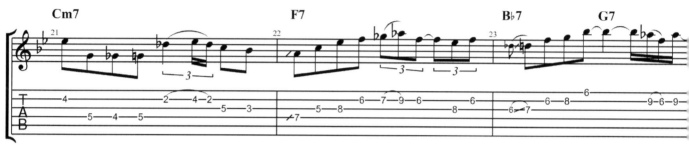

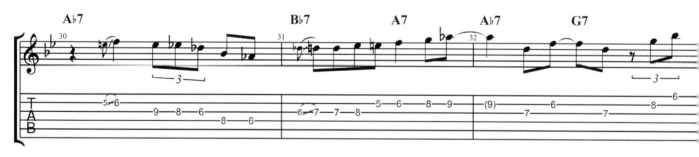

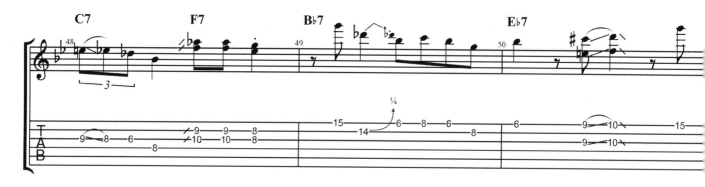

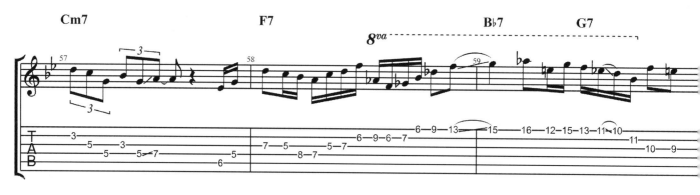

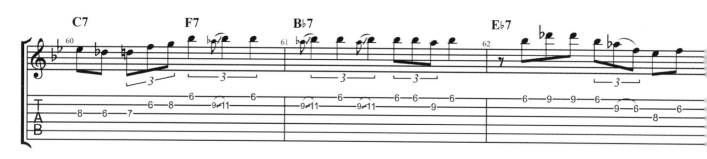

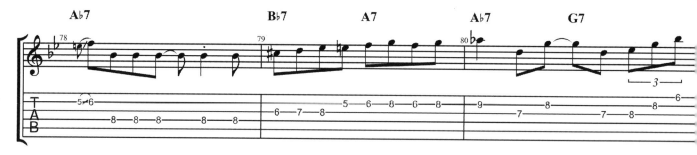

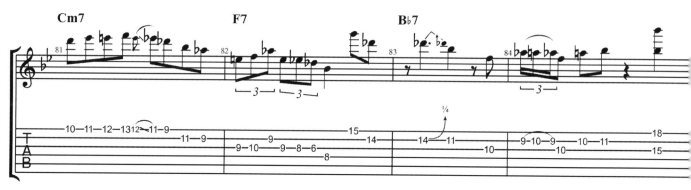

Etude 7

Based on the Rhythm Changes

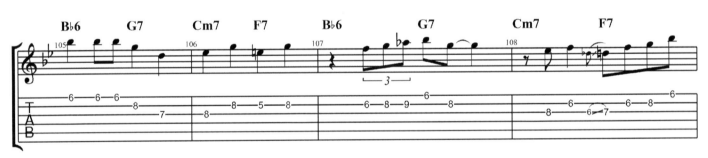

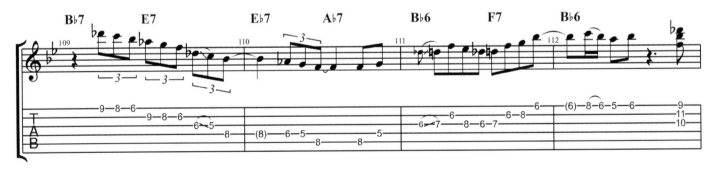

Etude 8

Based on *Jersey Bounce*

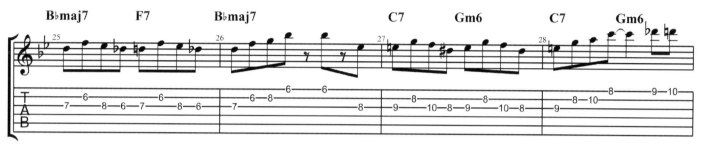

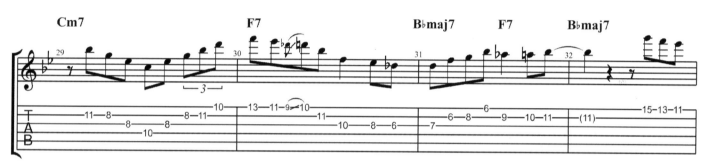

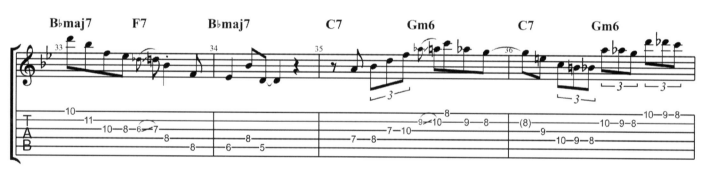

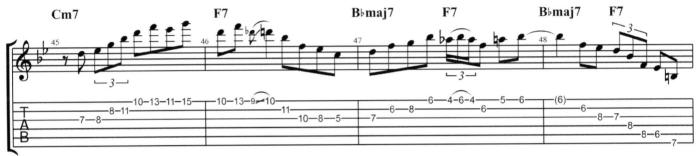

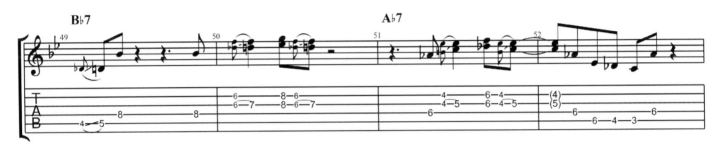

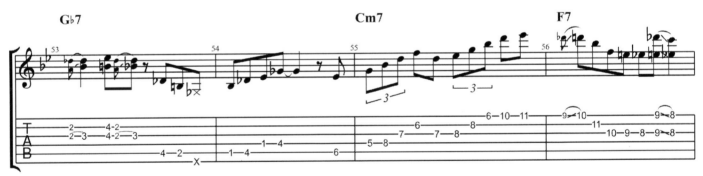

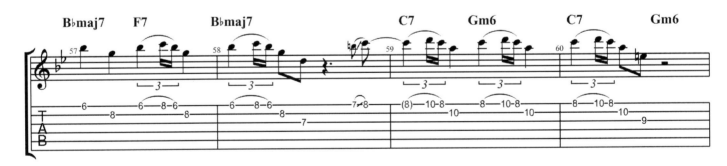

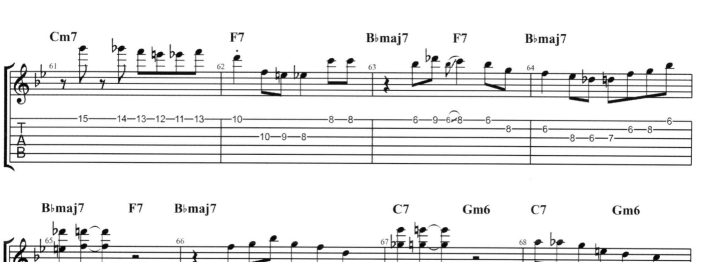

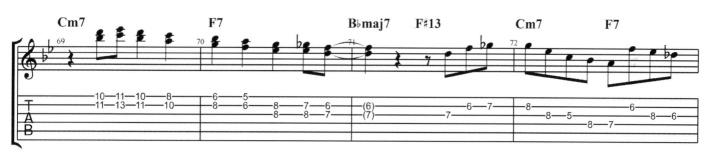

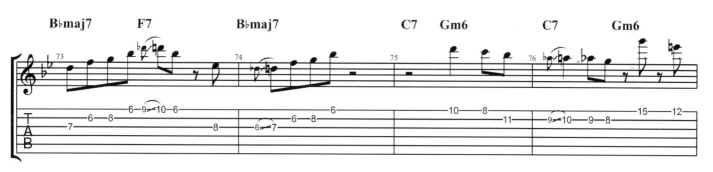

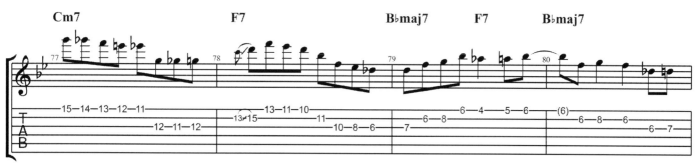

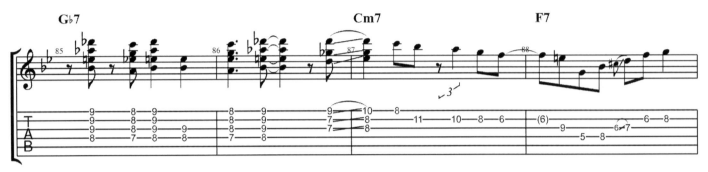

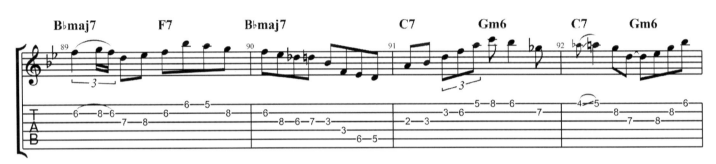

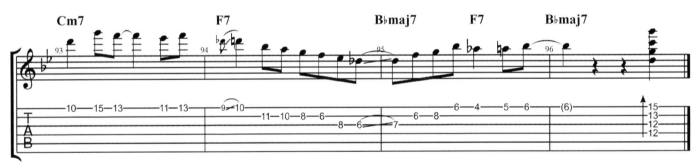

Etude 9

Based on *How High the Moon*

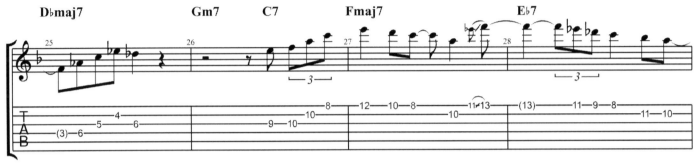

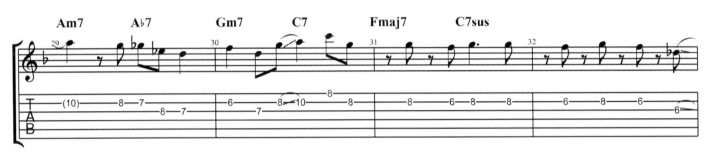

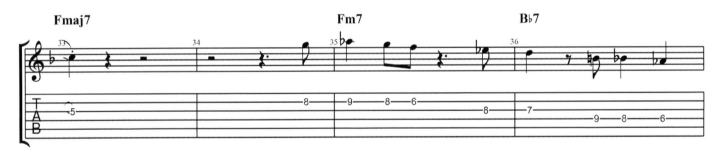

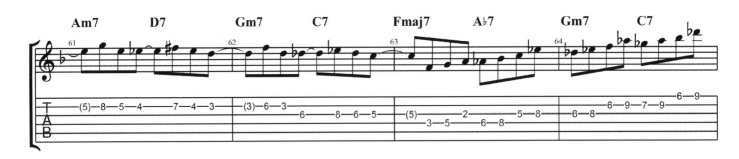

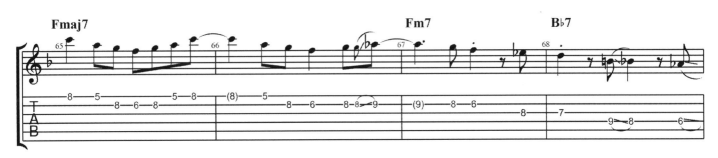

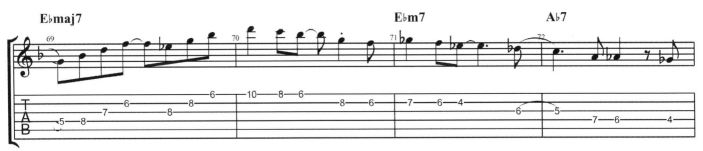

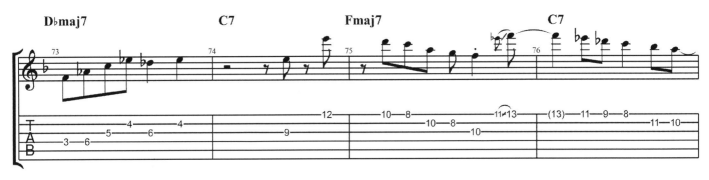

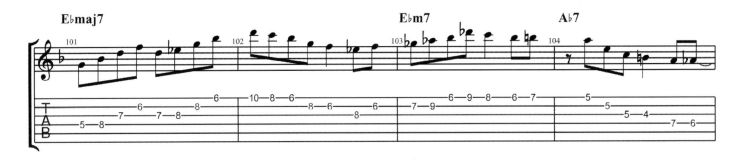
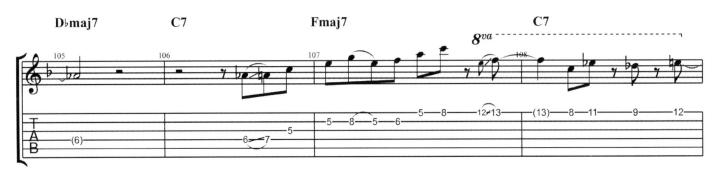

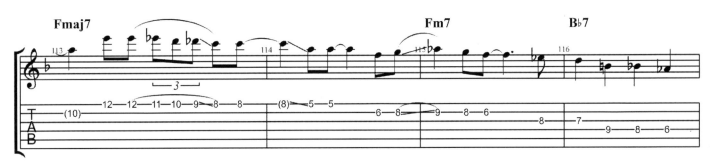
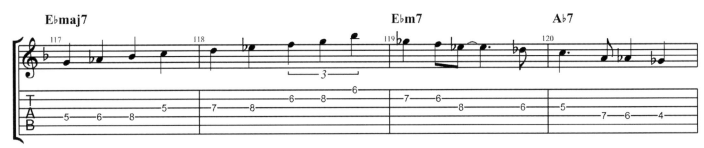

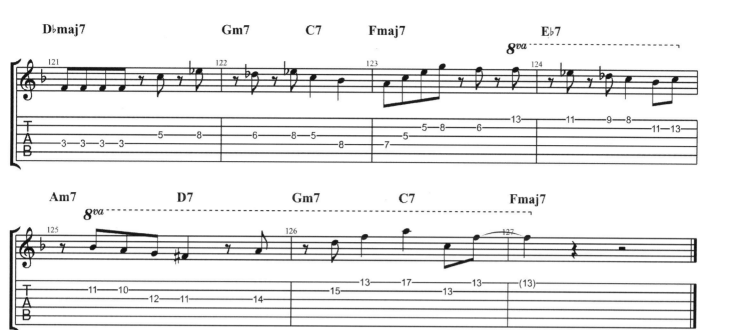

Etude 10

Based on *Georgia On My Mind*

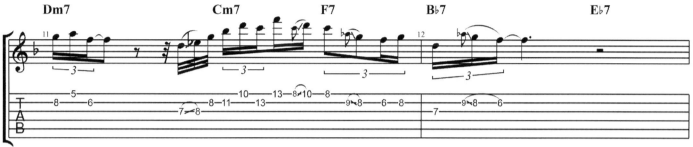

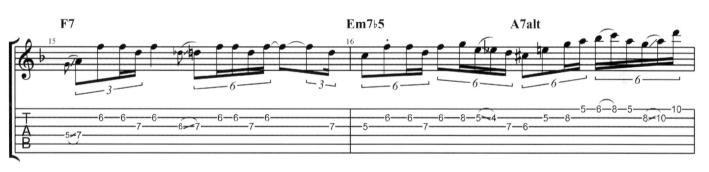

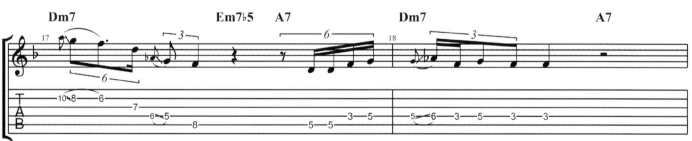

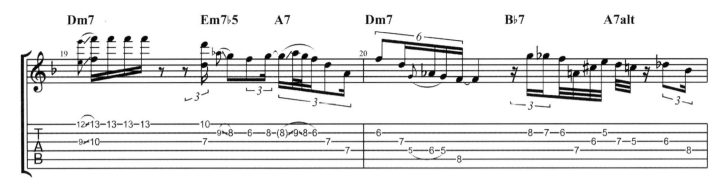

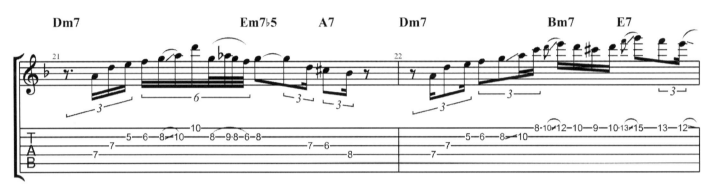

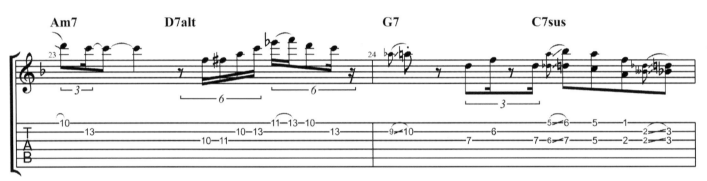

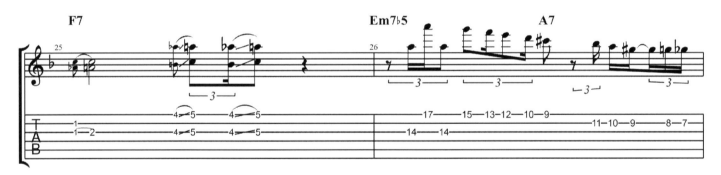

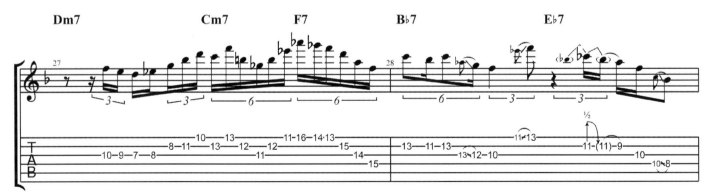

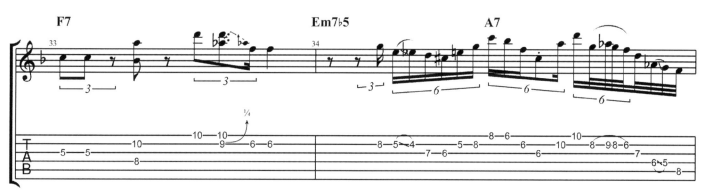

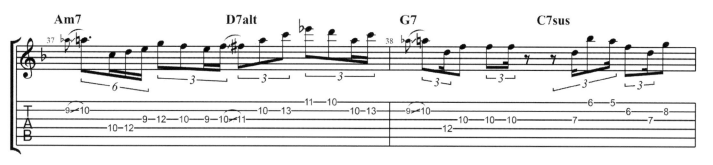

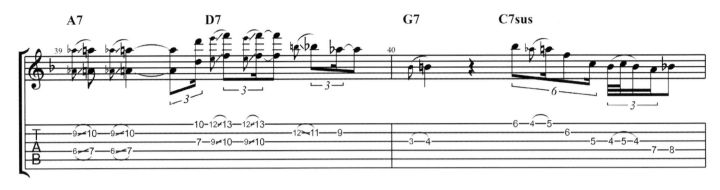

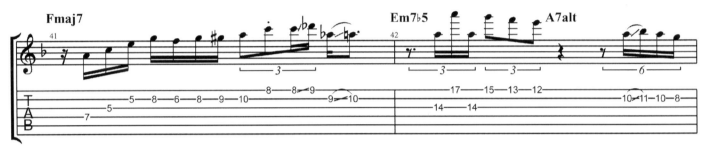

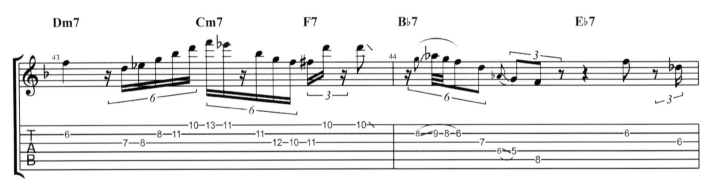

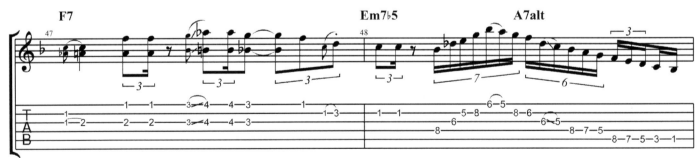

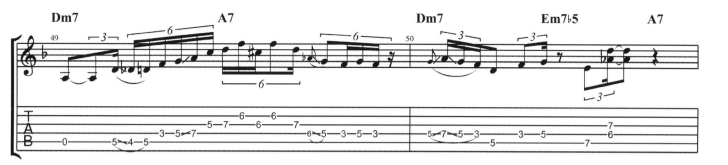

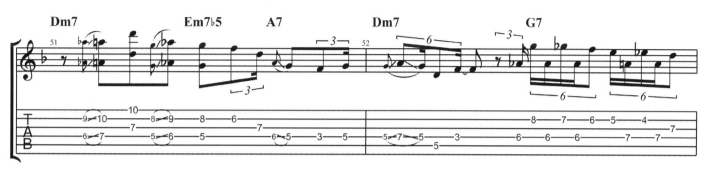

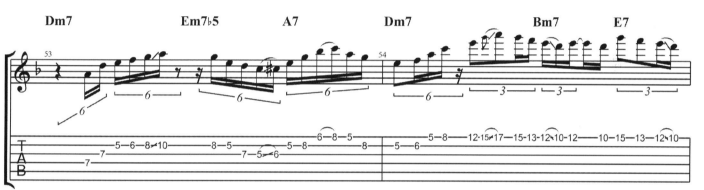

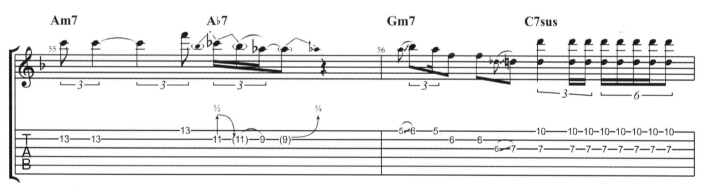

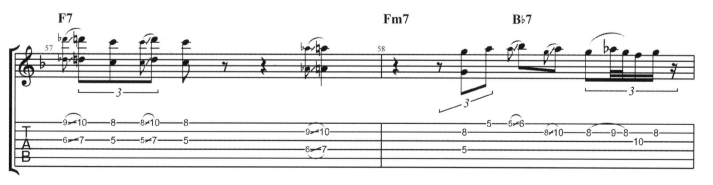

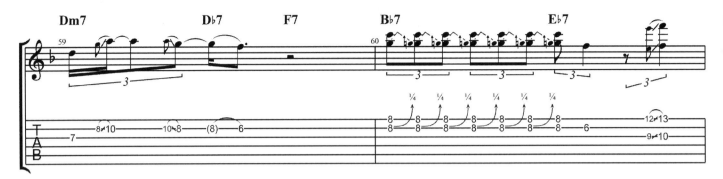

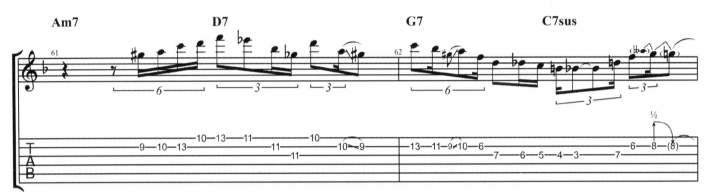

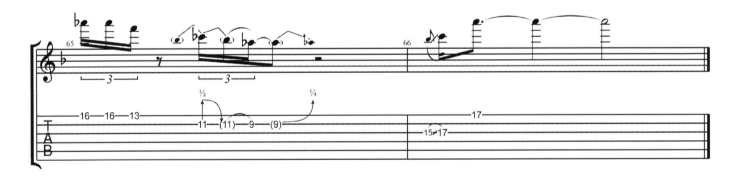

Etude 11

Based on *On Green Dolphin Street*

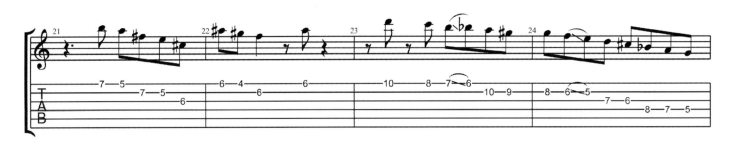

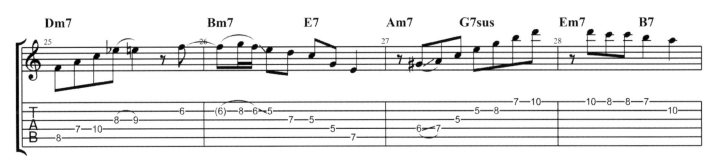

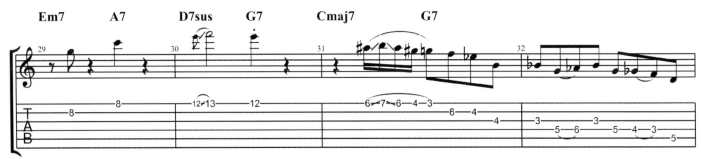

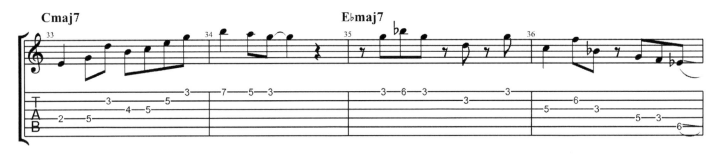

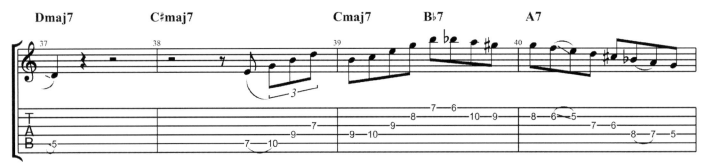

70

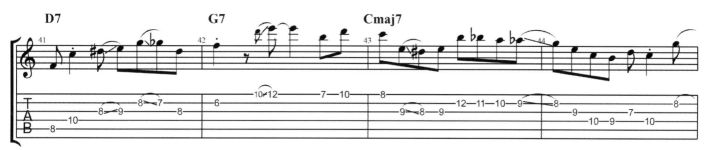

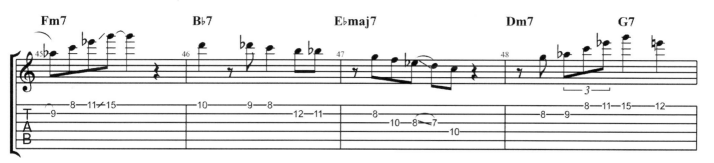

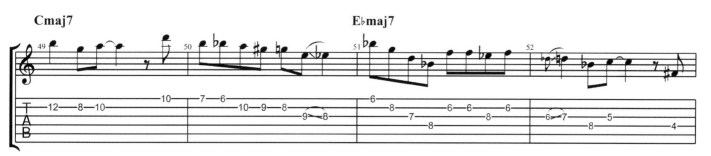

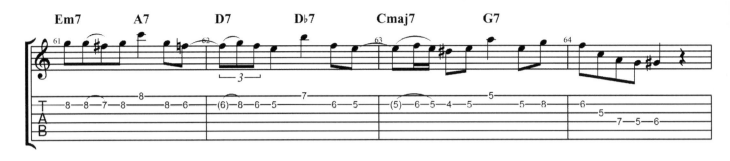

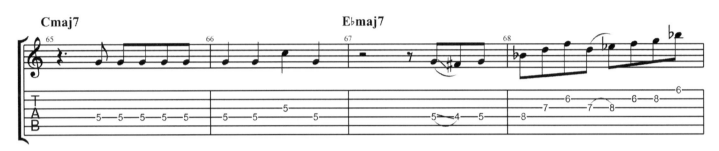

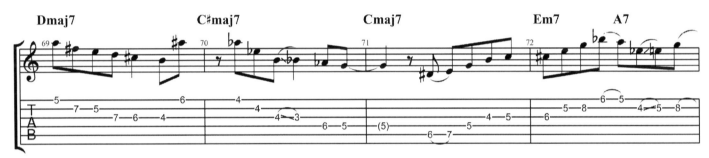

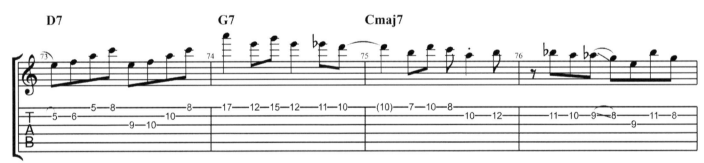

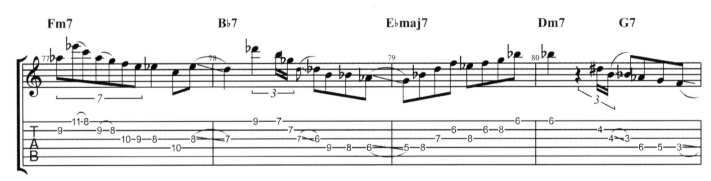

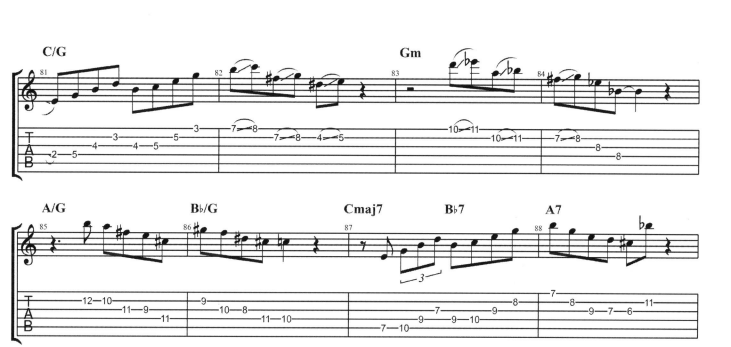

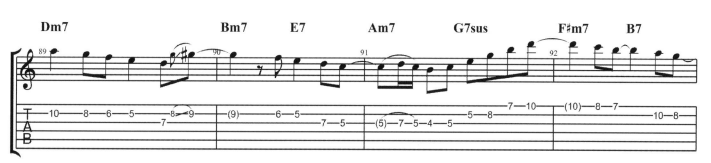

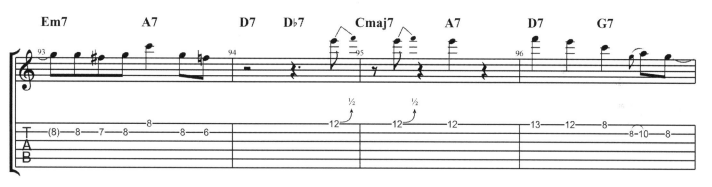

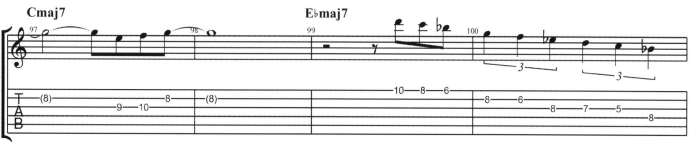

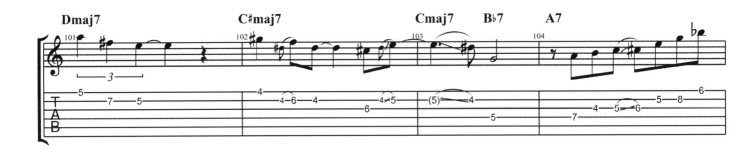

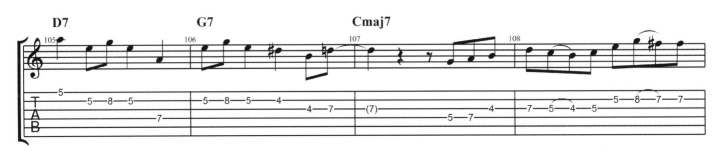

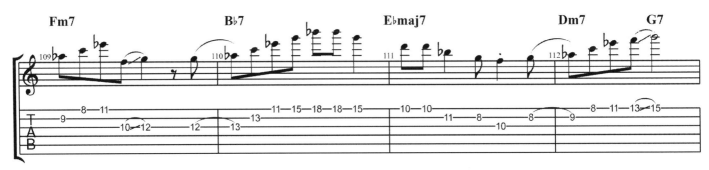

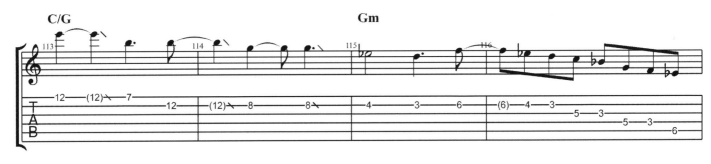

74

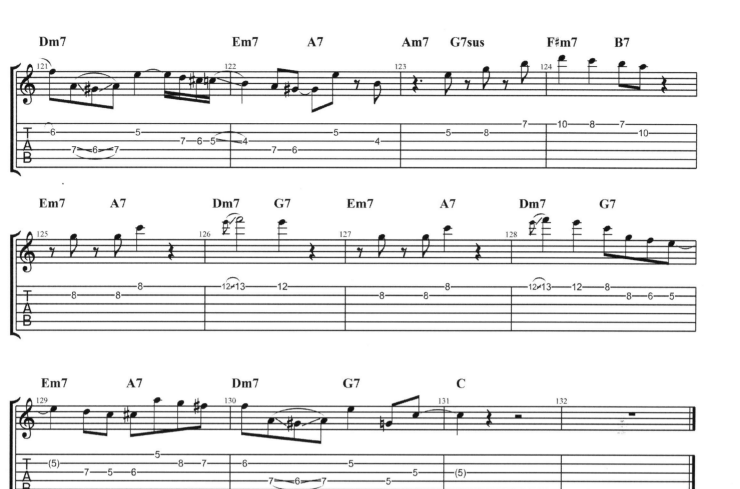

Etude 12

Based on *Emily*

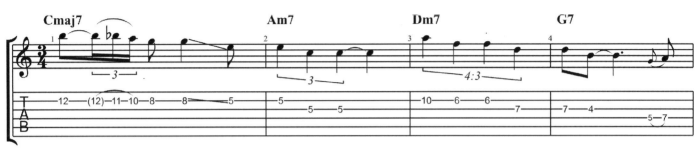

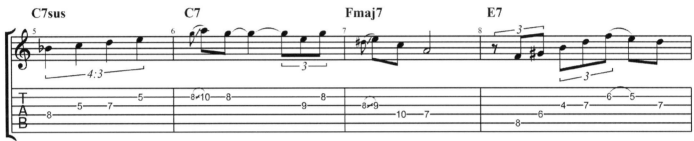

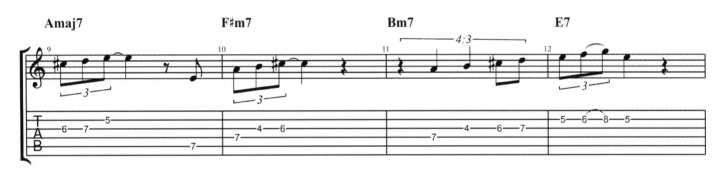

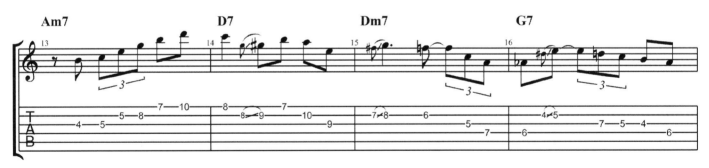

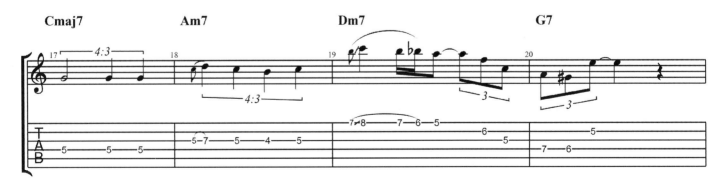

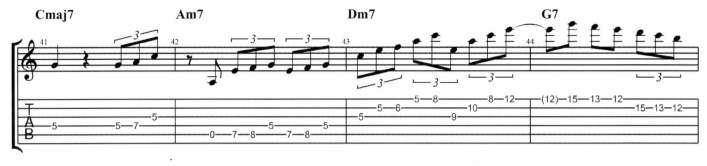

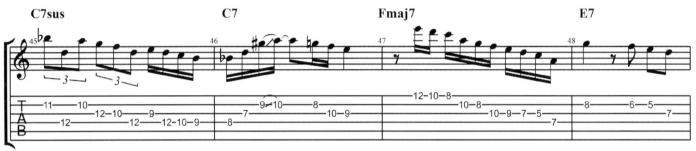

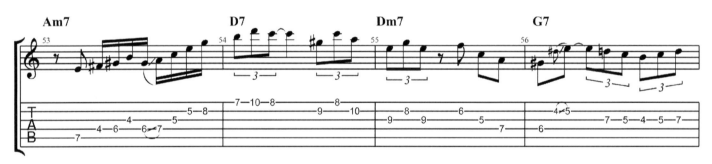

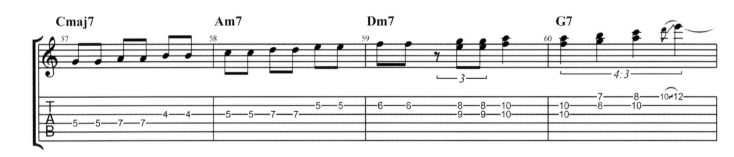

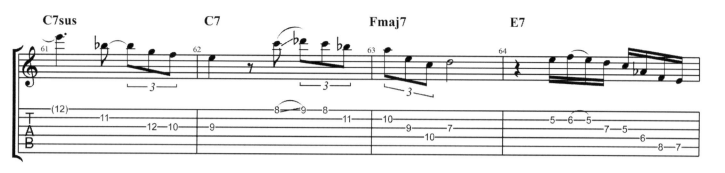

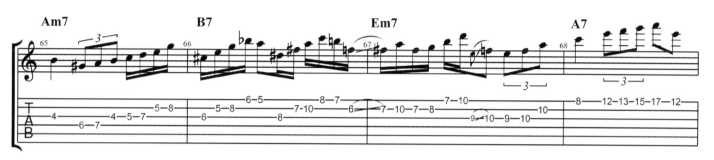

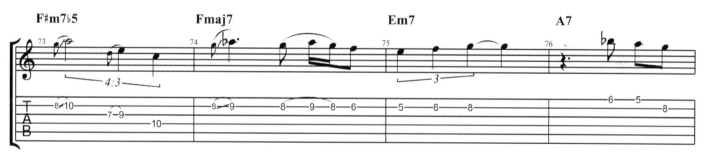

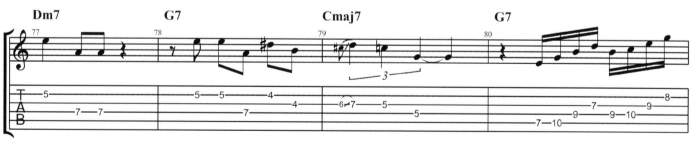

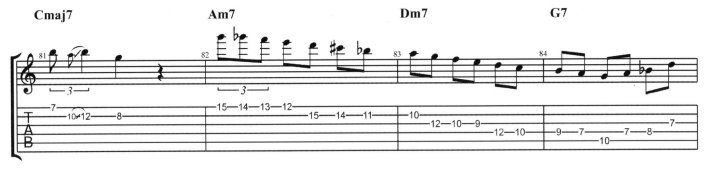

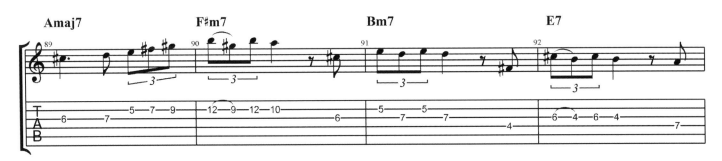

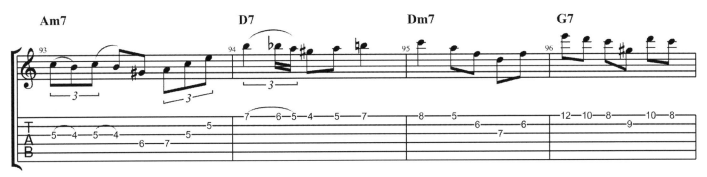

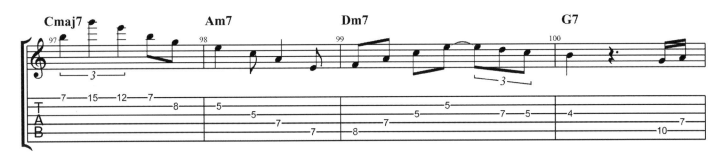

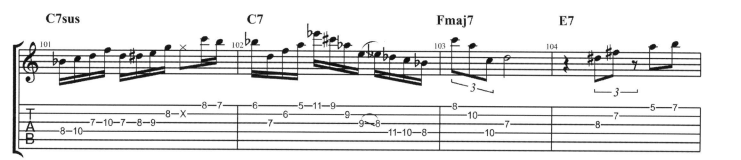

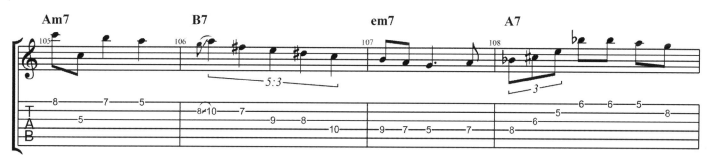

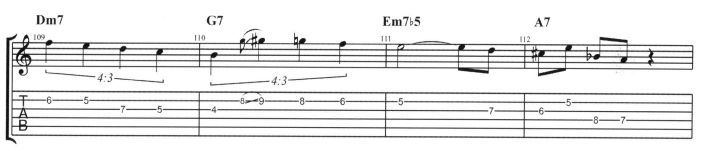

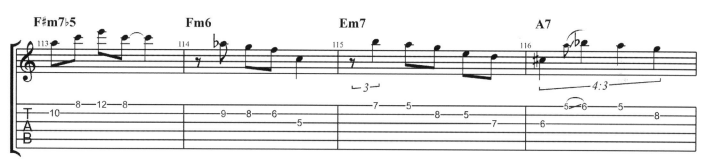

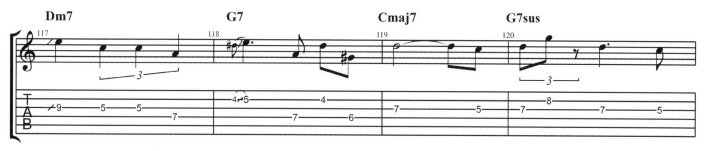

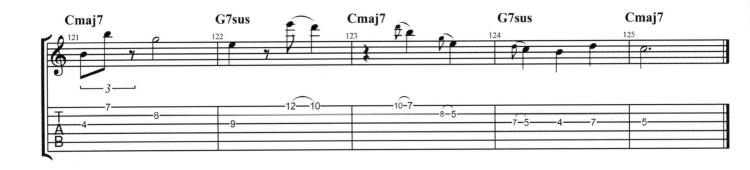

By the Same Author

Martin Taylor Beyond Chord Melody

- Master 7 steps to perfect jazz guitar chord melody

- Learn to create your own beautiful jazz guitar arrangements

- Discover Martin's secret approach to chord melody playing

Martin Taylor – Walking Bass for Jazz Guitar

- Learn walking baselines from the internationally acclaimed master of jazz guitar

- Discover how to effortlessly combine jazz chords and walking basslines

- Become the ultimate jazz rhythm guitar player and accompanist

Martin Taylor Single Note Soloing for Jazz Guitar

- Learn a time-honoured method for jazz improvisation that puts music before theory

- The Think, Sing, Play method that in time will lead you to be able to play any line you think of

- How to refine your jazz vocabulary and develop your phrasing

Martin Taylor's Complete Jazz Guitar Method Compilation

- Three best-selling jazz guitar books in one definitive edition:

Beyond Chord Melody

Walking Bass for Jazz Guitar

Single Note Soloing for Jazz Guitar

- With almost 300 pages and hundreds of musical examples, Martin Taylor takes you on a journey through his virtuoso approaches to chord melody guitar, combining basslines with chords, and how to really solo like a jazz guitar icon.

Martin Taylor's Christmas Songs for Jazz Guitar

- Learn Martin Taylor's Jazz Guitar Arrangements of 10 Beautiful Christmas Carols

- Complete with full notation, tablature, audio and insights into each piece from Martin, you'll discover a whole new versatile repertoire of Christmas songs, arranged for jazz guitar

Beginner/Intermediate Jazz Guitar Licks Phrasebook

An organised library of jazz guitar phrases

Over 100 jazz guitar licks distilled from five decades of guitar virtuosity

Intermediate/Advanced Jazz Guitar Licks Phrasebook

- A masterclass in developing motifs and perfect phrasing

- A guide to rhythmic phrasing, variation and articulation to build whole solos

- Live recorded audio examples from Martin Taylor's own studio

Printed in Great Britain
by Amazon